T0052774

PRIVATE•LESSONS

Classical Themes for Electric Guitar

25 Solo Guitar Arrangements

by Jean Marc Belkadi

ISBN 0-634-07012-6

7777 W. BLUEMOUND RD. P.O. BOX 13819 MILWAUKEE, WI 53213

In Australia Contact:
Hal Leonard Australia Pty. Ltd.
22 Taunton Drive P.O. Box 5130
Cheltenham East, 3192 Victoria, Australia
Email: ausadmin@halleonard.com

Visit Hal Leonard Online at
www.halleonard.com

Contents

Introduction

The purpose of this book is to achieve a classical sound on electric guitar, and understand, with the study of some memorable masterpieces from the past five centuries, the complexity of these composers' work. This is a fresh look at music from the past that will introduce new concepts for your performance and technique. The compositions are challenging in many aspects and great for the study of rhythm, melody, and especially counterpoint. Feel free to perform these with any effect you like: reverb, chorus, echo, etc. I encourage you to use a guitar synthesizer and try various sounds like voice, cello, string orchestra, and so on. Try it; it's great!

I wrote a small biography on each composer in the book. You will feel as though you are traveling through time and getting into their minds. That is what this book is all about—experiencing the music of the past with the sounds of today.

Renaissance Period (1400–1600)

Joachim van den Hove:	"Canarie"
Cesare Negri:	"Bianca Fiore"
John Dowland:	"Mrs. Nichol's Alman"

Guitars probably existed in very early civilization, but the first written evidence of the instrument appeared in one of the legends of ancient Greece. The guitar really started to take its shape around the twelfth century, influenced by small and practical musical instruments brought back to Europe from the crusades.

During the Renaissance, it evolved into what we know as the lute and vihuela (Spanish version of the lute). The lute was the favorite instrument of the fourteenth, fifteenth, and sixteenth centuries. But by the end of the sixteenth century, these aristocratic instruments gradually disappeared in favor of the already more popular guitar, which possessed a fourth course of strings. Most surviving Renaissance compositions were written for the lute, and the majority of the lute collection is from England. Many Renaissance paintings illustrate angels, aristocratic women, or mythological characters from antiquity playing the lute.

Joachim van den Hove (1567–1620)

Renaissance composer, lutenist, and teacher Joachim van den Hove was a contemporary of lutenist John Dowland. He was born in Antwerp, Netherlands in 1567. He hasn't quite fallen into obscurity thanks to his two anthologies of lute compositions, *Florida* (1601) and *Delitiae Musicae* (1612), and a third collection of pieces more devoted to his own compositions, *Praeludia Testudinis* (1616).

CANARIE

Track 1

Music by Joachim van den Hove

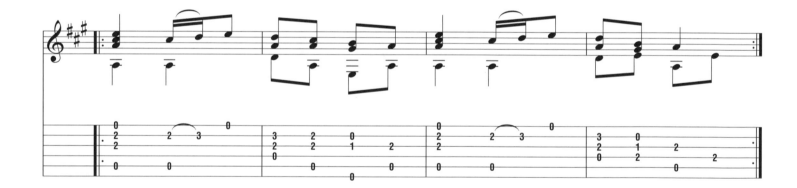

Cesare Negri (1535–1604)

Cesare Negri is most famous for two books, *Le Gratie d'Amore* and *Nuove Inventioni Di Balli*, both collections of dance songs and dance choreographies of the latter sixteenth century. No one knows if the songs were composed by him or by an unknown composer of his era. "Bianca Fiore" ("White Flower") is the most famous and beautiful song of the two compilations.

BIANCA FIORE

Track 2

Music by Cesare Negri

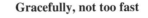
Drop D tuning:
(low to high) D-A-D-G-B-E

Gracefully, not too fast

John Dowland (1563–1626)

John Dowland was a renowned English composer of the sixteenth century. His music was melancholic, elegant, and moving. He was one of the rare English lutenists to be recognized all over Europe during his lifetime, but his fame gradually faded over the next two centuries. It was only in the early twentieth century that he was rediscovered by lute scholars, but most of his compositions are still not published, and only a small number of lute enthusiasts know about them.

He traveled the courts of Europe, living in France for four years where he converted to Catholicism. He then came back to the court of Elizabeth of England, but feeling unwelcome because of his new faith, he left for Rome to study with Luca Marenzio. He then lived in Germany and Denmark before coming back to England, laden with debts. In 1612, he published his last book for voice and lute, *A Pilgrimes Solace*, and was appointed to the King's Lutes.

MRS. NICHOL'S ALMAN

Track 3

Music by John Dowland

BAROQUE PERIOD (1600–1750)

Robert de Visée:	"Serenade"
Johann Krieger:	"Bourree in B Minor"
Georg Philipp Telemann:	"Minuet"
Johann Sebastian Bach:	"Aria"
Jean-Philippe Rameau:	"Rondeau I"
George Frideric Handel:	"Gavotte"
Henry Purcell:	"Air"

The lute had a problem with its tuning, which affected the virtuosity and technique of the players. It seemed they spent more time tuning than playing. So during the Baroque years, all sorts of keyboards became more practical. Violins and other stringed instruments also took a more prominent place. Meanwhile, the guitar continued its evolution, and a fifth course was added during the seventeenth century. The Baroque years reflected the exuberance of the aristocratic society with a highly structured and decorated music. The composers were employed by the numerous courts of Europe, which were artistically competing with each other. The result was a very flamboyant style requested by the princes who wanted to show the world their wealth and power.

This period in music, more than any other, gave the performer a great freedom of interpretation. The composer wrote a basic score described as a skeleton, and the performer added the musical ornamentation according to his inspiration. Bach was the greatest improvisator of the time.

New forms of music were written, such as canons, fugues, and variations. New harmonies (Jean-Philippe Rameau) and combinations of instruments were explored as well. The complexity of the counterpoint style is fundamental to the period, and Bach, Telemann, and Krieger mesmerized their audiences with this technique.

Robert de Visée (1660–1725)

Little is known about the life of Robert de Visée, but he is remembered as the French court of Versailles' guitarist and singer. He served as guitar teacher to Louis XIV and Dauphin's until 1721 (when he left the position to his son) and performed for the glamorous parties of the aristocracy and royal events. He composed many suites for the baroque guitar, which had five pairs (or courses) of strings at the time; his most famous one was *The Suite in D Minor* (1686). He also wrote three books: the *Livre de Guitare Dedié au Roy* (Paris, 1682), the *Livre de Pièces pour la Guitare Dedié au Roy* (1686), and the *Pièces de Théorbe et de Luth Mises en Partition* (1716). Altogether, he left a legacy of 189 pieces.

SERENADE

Track 4

Music by Robert de Visée

Johann Krieger (1651–1735)

German organist Johann Krieger is most famous for his contrapuntal technique and his huge influence on Bach. He is said to be the best contrapuntist of the seventeenth and eighteenth centuries. Handel and Mattheson were among his many admirers. His brother Johann Philipp was also a composer of great fame and composed more than 2200 church cantatas. Johann also composed a prodigious amount of works, but only a small number survived. The rest have been destroyed and forgotten. He served as an organist in Zittau, Germany from 1682 until the end of his life.

BOURRÉE IN B MINOR

Track 5

Music by Johann Krieger

Georg Philipp Telemann (1681–1767)

Georg Telemann grew up in a family of clergymen. He fell in love with music at a very young age and learned it mostly on his own. He mastered several instruments (violin, keyboard, and flute) and composed his first opera, *Sigismundus*, at the age of twelve.

In 1701, under pressure from his family, he put music aside for a while in order to study law and science at the university of Leipzig in Germany. It didn't last long, and within the first year, he founded the Student Collegium Musicum. A year later, he was appointed musical director of the Leipzig Opera. In 1705, he took the position of Kapellmeister at the court of Zary. He moved on to Eisenach in 1708 and Frankfurt in 1712. During this period he wrote and published many cantatas, chamber music, and oratorios. All along he went on writing operas for the Leipzig Opera.

Telemann was very good friends with Bach and in 1714, Bach asked him to be the godfather of his son Carl Philipp Emmanuel. Their paths crossed several times, and in 1722 he was selected over Bach to be the Cantor of the Leipzig Tomaskirche, but due to his responsibilities as musical director of the five most important churches in Hamburg, he was not able to accept the position. He stayed in Hamburg for the rest of his life and was succeeded by his godson Carl Philipp Emmanuel Bach when he died in 1767.

He is considered one of the most important German composers and was also very wealthy; his salary was three times higher than Bach's. Telemann was also a friend of Handel, who joked about his prolificness as a composer, saying that Telemann could write compositions as easily as letters. Telemann wrote about 1043 church cantatas, twenty operas, 600 orchestral suites, forty-six passions, and more.

MINUET

Track 6

Music by Georg Philipp Telemann

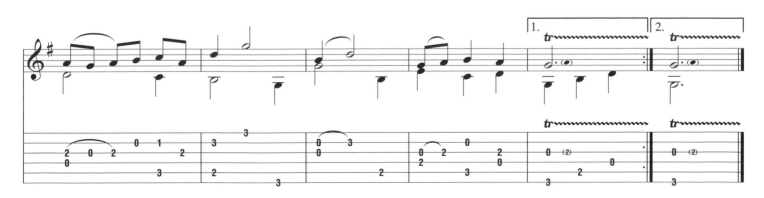

Johann Sebastian Bach (1685–1750)

Bach came from a dynasty of composers. Four of his sons were also composers and actually become more famous than he was during their lifetimes. Paradoxically, the world became interested in Johann Sebastian Bach's compositions (over 1,000 of them) a century after his death, while his sons' works became less appreciated with the passing of time. Nevertheless, he was during his life highly regarded as a master organist and great improviser.

Bach was born in Germany on March 21, 1685 and was raised by his brother Johann Christoph, himself a musician, from whom Bach learned the fundamentals. In 1703 Bach secured his first musical position in Weimar, where he would eventually serve as the court organist for nine years. He composed many cantatas and most of his organ pieces there, including the famous "Orgel-Büchlein." He never did attain the position of Kapellmeister, however, because he chose to compose pieces for the Weimar Regent's aristocratic rival. Bach was eventually jailed for a month as a consequence. Around 1707, he married his first wife, Maria Barbara.

Bach finally found his desperately sought-after Kapellmeister position in Cothen around 1717. He worked there until the marriage of the prince in 1723, after which little focus was placed on music. In 1721 Bach married Anna Magdalena, a gifted soprano, after the sudden death of his first wife. They moved to Leipzig in 1723, where he would spend the rest of his life. Over the next twenty-seven years, as Kapellmeister of the Saint Thomas church, he composed his most complex body of baroque work. Bach was highly respected by the Leipzig aristocratic society and often visited by famous musicians eager to hear his latest compositions, such as *A Musical Offering* and *The Art of the Fugue*—both masterpieces of counterpoint.

Bach died of a stroke on July 28, 1750. He is remembered for the *Canonic Variations*, the *Goldberg Variations*, and of course his supreme mastery of counterpoint and the fugue form.

ARIA

Music by Johann Sebastian Bach

Track 7

Moderato

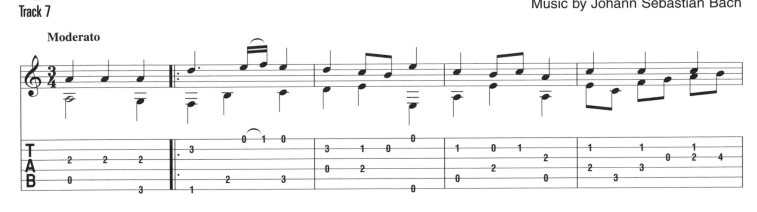

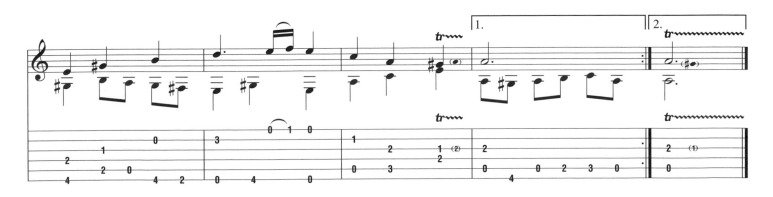

Jean-Philippe Rameau (1683–1764)

Jean-Philippe Rameau was taught music by his father, a professional organist at the St. Etienne Cathedral in Dijon, France. In 1702, Jean-Philippe became a music master at the Cathedral of Notre Dame of Avignon. He moved to Clermont for a while before settling in Paris in 1706. There, he published his first book, *Premier livre de pièces de clavecin*, but in 1709, he came back to Dijon to replace his father at Notre Dame until 1713. He moved to Paris in 1722 to publish his famous *Traité de l'harmonie*. It would be followed in 1726 by *Le nouveau système de musique thorium*.

Rameau is regarded as a great theoretician of music. He is one of the first to think of music as a science and developed the concept that music is based on harmony, with all chords derived from the perfect minor and major triads and the 7th chord. He formulated the concept of harmony inversion and invented the concept of a fundamental bass. His musical concepts are still studied and are the backbone of tonal harmony.

Among other theoretical books, he wrote *Génération harmonique* in 1737, *Démonstration du principe de l'harmonie* (co-written with Diderot) in 1750, and *Observations sur notre instinct pour la musique* in 1752. Meanwhile D'Alembert gathered Rameau's theories in a book titled *Eléments de musique théorique et pratique* (1752).

Rameau was highly admired by other musicians, but his theories were questioned and not quite immediately accepted. He became famous for many polemics about harmony with Rousseau, Diderot, D'Alembert, and Grimm. He only started to compose for the opera at the age of fifty. *Hippolyte et Arecie* (1733) was his first opera, followed by *Les Indes gallantes* in 1735 and *Castor et Pollux* in 1737. He also wrote many publications for harpsichord. When he died in 1764, thousands attended his funeral.

Track 8

RONDEAU I

Music by Jean-Philippe Rameau

George Frideric Handel (1685–1759)

Handel's father raised him to become a lawyer, but Handel was more interested in being a musician. He started to display musical talent around the age of seven, and his father let him study music with the city of Halle music director.

When his father died, he completely abandoned law in favor of music. In 1703, he moved to Hamburg, Germany, the center of the European opera. There he composed *The Passion According to St. John* (1704) and his first opera, *Almira* (1705), while serving as the second violinist of the Opera House. He left Hamburg for Italy, where he would build the foundation of his style and deepen his love for the opera. Between 1706 and 1710, he composed brilliant operas and cantatas inspired by the Italian composers and the beauty of Rome, Florence, Naples, and Venice.

After a brief stay in Hanover, he moved to England in 1712. King George I appointed him music director of the Royal Court, and Handel thanked him with *Water Music* in 1717. Three years later, a group of Aristocrats impressed by Handel created the Royal Academy of Music in his honor. Until 1728, he composed successful Italian operas, among them *Giulio Cesare* (1724), but his success faded, and the company had to close its doors due to the public's loss of interest in opera. He took over the London theater house, changed the direction of his writing, and created a new genre: the English oratorio with *Saul*, *Israel in Egypt* (1739), and his most famous, *Messiah*, performed in Dublin in 1742. He went on composing revered works such as *Samson*, *Joshua*, *Solomon*, and *Jephtra* (1752), but his progressive blindness eventually took its toll on his work.

Along with J.S. Bach, Handel is considered the great master of the Baroque Period. He died an English citizen at the age of 74, as he had made England his permanent residence thirty-three years before his death. He was buried in Westminster Abbey in the presence of 3000 admirers.

GAVOTTE

Track 9

Music by George Frideric Handel

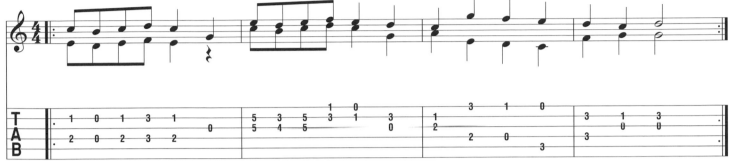

Henry Purcell (1659–1695)

Henry Purcell is one of the giants of the Baroque era and probably the greatest English composer. He was a chorister at the Chapel Royal, where he studied with Blow, whom he replaced as organist at Westminster Abbey in 1679. Blow would come back to his position after Purcell's early death in 1695. Purcell's composing for the stage may be traced to 1680; he would eventually write music for more than forty plays. In 1682, he became organist at the Chapel Royal and composed the opera *Dido and Aeneas.* He was a versatile musician, contributing his talent to many styles of music. He wrote cantatas for solo voices, orchestral, and chamber music. Purcell also composed many duets and more than 150 songs. He was buried at Westminster Abbey, where the music he had composed ten months earlier for the funeral of Queen Mary II was played.

AIR

Track 10

Music by Henry Purcell

3 CLASSICAL PERIOD (1750–1820)

Mauro Guiliani:	"Balkan Skies"
Joseph Kuffner:	"Andante in D Major"
Franz Joseph Haydn:	"Minuet" from *Symphony No. 104*
Wolfgang Amadeus Mozart:	"Prelude," "Andante"
Ludwig van Beethoven:	*Piano Concerto No. 3, Opus 37* – First Movement, Second Theme

During the Classical years, the composer became more in control of his own music, and the performer had to follow the score as written. The counterpoint and the embellished style were replaced by a more stylish sophistication. The music became more emotional and elegant. The composer researched simplicity and structural clarity.

Non-commissioned compositions flourished, as the quest for the composer's own individuality and intellectual freedom became the main ideal. He no longer wanted to compose upon request, instead preferring a spontaneous approach. New forms of instrumental orchestrations emerged once again, such as the concerto and symphony.

The trio sonata (strings) evolved into the modern string quartet, and sonatas for piano, violin, and cello became the flavors of the day. The role of instruments changed. The harpsichord became a solo instrument, the piano and violin were added, and the European courts appreciated the compositions performed on the refined guitar of the eighteenth century. The double courses were converted into single strings, and a sixth string was added above the other five.

Mauro Giuliani (1781–1829)

Born in 1781 in Bisceglie, Italy, Mauro Giuliani is one of the greatest guitarists of the nineteenth century. He learned cello and violin before guitar became his first real passion. He quickly developed a prodigious technique on the guitar, and his virtuosity allowed him to perform all over Europe. He eventually settled down in Vienna, Austria, where he established the biggest European guitarist community. There, he played the first performance of the *Sixth Symphony*, composed and conducted by the most prominent composer of the time, Beethoven.

He was so famous as a guitarist that a magazine known as *The Guilianiad* was published to celebrate his playing and compositions. He wrote more than 150 pieces and excelled in the "theme and variations" form. He wrote the *Variations over Handel's Suite No. 5 in F Major* for harpsichord. He was also an eminent teacher and wrote a guitar method called *Studio per la Chitarra*.

In 1819, he returned to Rome, Italy and met Rossini. Bored, he left for Naples to be closer to his father, where he gave numerous concerts with one of his daughters, Emilia—also a guitar virtuoso. Giuliani continued composing and performing until his death in May 1829.

BALKAN SKIES

Track 11

Music by Mauro Giuliani

Joseph Kuffner (1776–1856)

German violinist and guitarist Joseph Kuffner was one of the most famous court musicians of his time. His celebrity was even greater than that of his friend and contemporary Beethoven, though his compositions were never considered as important.

He wrote many short duets for guitar and about thirty songs that serve as excellent studies for the guitar. He was a prolific composer, and an arranger for Verdi, with over 300 compositions for opera, chamber music, and duets for clarinets, piano, violin, and guitar.

ANDANTE IN D MAJOR

Music by Joseph Kuffner

Track 12

Copyright © 2004 by HAL LEONARD CORPORATION
International Copyright Secured   All Rights Reserved

Franz Joseph Haydn (1732–1809)

Born in Austria in 1732, Franz Joseph Haydn was raised to become a wheelwright like his father until he displayed some vocal talents at a young age. His music-loving father sent the eight-year-old Franz Joseph to be part of the St. Stephen Cathedral Vienna Boys Choir. A few years later his brother Michael (1737–1806) followed the same steps—a unique educational opportunity for poor children. At the school choir they learned to play keyboard, harpsichord, organ, and violin, and studied Latin. Michael, who befriended Mozart, also became a respected composer and had a flourishing musical career, but he never achieved a level of notoriety like Franz Joseph's.

When Haydn's voice reached puberty, he was dismissed from the choir and had to earn a living. He had the chance, after a few years of giving music lessons, to enter the aristocratic house of the Prince Paul Esterházy as a Kapellmeister. For the next twenty-nine years, he composed for the family over 100 symphonies, two oratorios, fifty-eight piano sonatas, and many masses, cantatas, and concertos that would establish him as a master of the classical form and one of the highest regarded composers ever. For Prince Paul Esterházy alone, who loved to perform for his own court, he composed 125 trios.

When Prince Esterházy died, Haydn was authorized by the family to travel only to England and Paris, where he published and performed new works that earned him an international reputation. He went back to the Palace of Esterháza in 1795 to compose and play for the son and grandson of Paul Esterházy. After many years under the security of the famous aristocratic family, he was finally awarded some freedom and lived most of his last years in Vienna. Mozart was one of his students, and many composers would visit him. He died in 1809 during the French occupation. He was so respected that Napoleon, who had invaded the Austrian Capital, gave in person his last respects to the great composer. Haydn was a major influence on generations of great classical masters like Fernando Sor and Mauro Giuliani, even though he never composed for guitar.

MINUET FROM SYMPHONY NO. 104

Track 13

Music by Franz Joseph Haydn

Drop D tuning:
(low to high) D-A-D-G-B-E

Andante

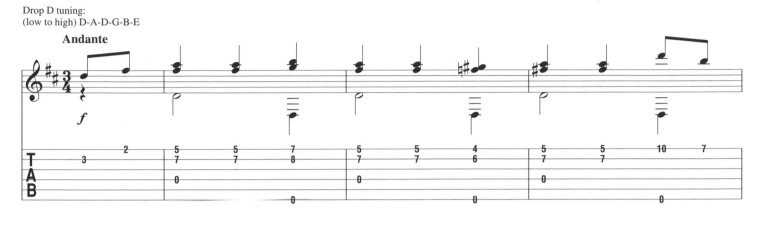

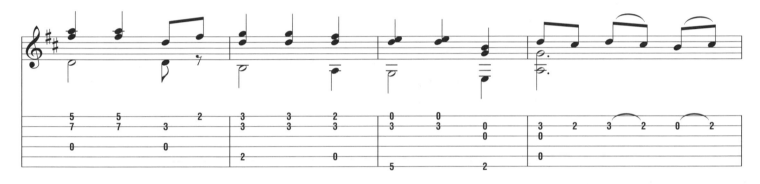

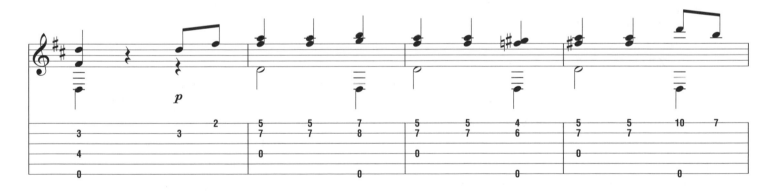

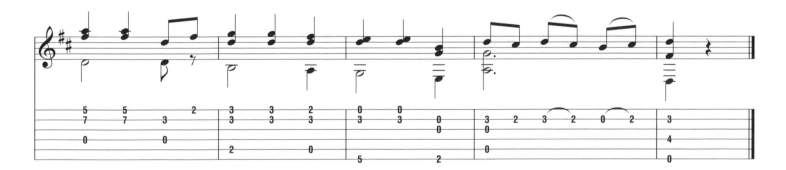

Wolfgang Amadeus Mozart (1756–1791)

Mozart was born Jan. 27, 1756 in Salzburg, Austria. He was a child prodigy and excelled in music at an early age. By the age of five he played harpsichord and piano to perfection. His father, also a very talented composer and violinist at the Salzburg court, decided to showcase his gifted children around the European courts. His older sister Maria Ana was also an accomplished pianist, and both children dazzled their royal audiences.

The extraordinary musical intelligence and composing that Wolfgang exhibited so young has never been quite equaled. He is possibly the greatest genius that the world of music has ever known. He composed minuets at the age of five, symphonies at nine, and at age twelve he wrote his first opera. His surrealistic genius was confirmed after a visit to the Vatican with his father Leopold on Easter Day of 1770. During a fifteen-month tour of Italy, he heard in the Sistine Chapel Gregorio Allegri's *Miserere*, a piece so sacred that the Vatican banned its performance outside its walls. Anybody who would copy the heavenly masterpiece would be excommunicated. Young Mozart is said to have transcribed it note for note and demonstrated such an incredibly perfect ear and musical memory that the Church, amazed, never dared excommunicate him.

At age fifteen, he became the concertmaster for the Archbishop of Salzburg. Under his protection, Mozart wrote sacred music, but alienated the Archbishop with his erratic behavior. He went on performing around Europe, mainly for the French and Italian courts. He came back to Salzburg in 1779, where he found a stable position as court organist and composed beautiful works until 1781, when he again lost the position due to his lack of professionalism.

In 1782, he was commissioned to work for the Vienna court, where he began writing the greatest masterpieces in classical music history. These pieces are so powerful that they are still performed on a daily basis around the world. The same year he married Constanze Weber, who bore him six children; sadly, only two survived. The younger, Franz Xaver Wolfgang, was also an excellent musician, but never achieved the notoriety of his father.

After his opera *The Marriage of Figaro* in 1786, he was not as well received at the court anymore due to the revolutionary views reflected in the work. 1789 marked the French revolution, and all the European royalty felt threatened by these democratic ideas. He started to struggle with a lot of debts and failing health, and in 1791 he was commissioned a requiem that he never finished.

He died on Dec. 5, 1791 of rheumatic fever at age thirty-five and was buried in a mass grave in Saint Marx, a village outside Vienna. His body is lost forever, but his music will stay in the heart of people for eternity. His student and friend Franz Xaver Süssmayr is believed to have completed the Requiem to help Constanze pay off some debts.

No words can describe Mozart's legacy. His achievements are prodigious, to say the least: 626 compositions divided in twenty-four categories, including forty-one symphonies and twenty-one operas.

PRELUDE

Music by Wolfgang Amadeus Mozart

Track 14

ANDANTE

Music by Wolfgang Amadeus Mozart

Track 15

Ludwig van Beethoven (1770–1827)

Beethoven was born in 1770 in Bonn, Germany. Like Mozart, he developed a tremendous musical talent at a very young age. He had his first work published at twelve, but his father failed to establish him as a young musical phenomenon.

At seventeen he moved to Vienna but had to come back to Bonn to bury his mother. He returned to Vienna five years later and settled there for the rest of his life with his two younger brothers. Beethoven made his brilliant public debut there in 1795, where he preferred the private performances of the aristocratic salons. He quickly earned the respect of high society, and word spread quickly of his piano virtuosity. In 1800 he participated in an improvisation contest and challenged the greatest pianist of the time, Daniel Steibelt.

Between 1792 and 1802, his composing, mainly for the piano, reflected the influence of his very critical teacher Haydn, with whom he had differences of opinion about music. During these years, he composed the *Pathetique* (1799) and *Moonlight* (1800) sonatas, which are very innovative and intense in style, three piano concertos, two symphonies (1800–1802), his first six string quartets, and a ballet called *The Creatures of Prometheus* (1801).

In a letter to his brothers in 1802, he revealed his worst feelings about his recent impaired hearing. In fact, his concerns regarding this affliction at the time were more social than musical. At this time he entered a new creative phase deemed the "middle period" by scholars. Between 1803 and 1812 his work turned out to be dramatic and tormented. He composed four more powerful symphonies, the *Eroica* (1803), the *Fourth* (1806), the *Fifth* (1805–1807), and the *Sixth* (1807–1808), the opera *Fidelio* (1803–1805), the *Violin Concerto* (1806), Goethe's drama *Egmont* (1810), and the famous "Für Elise" (1810).

The late period of his work was more introspective, and his progressive hearing loss culminated in a deep depression. He communicated with others through "conversation books" and had to stop performing in public. Nevertheless, he composed the *Seventh* (1811), *Eighth* (1812), and the commanding *Ninth* (1818) symphonies, a group of string quartets, and seven piano sonatas. Beethoven was the greatest composer of his time and impacted generations of music lovers and composers. His memorial service on March 26, 1827 was attended by 20,000 people.

PIANO CONCERTO NO. 3, OPUS 37
FIRST MOVEMENT, SECOND THEME

Track 16

Music by Ludwig van Beethoven

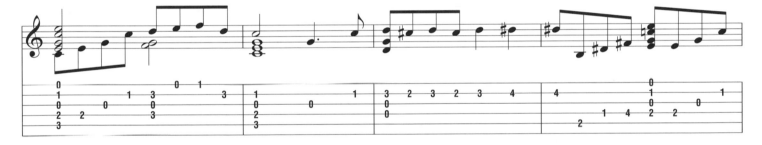

4 ROMANTIC PERIOD (1820–1910)

Franz Schubert :	"Two Ecossaises"
Johannes Brahms:	"Waltz," *Opus 39, No. 9*
Frederic Chopin:	"Prelude," *Opus 28, No. 7*
Robert Schumann:	"Melody"

In the Romantic period, the individualism of the Classical era intensified, and the composers looked to other artistic fields to find inspiration. The writers and poets of the day had a significant influence on composers, and a new style of symphony surfaced known as the symphonic poem. The music lost its previous formal abstraction in favor of a more lyrical and melodic structure. Emotion is the dominating theme of the romantic musicians. To express the powerful emotional moods, they used massive and colorful orchestration, added a wider variety of instruments, profusely used diminished seventh chords for modulation, and started to use dissonance and innovative chromatic alterations. Instruments used for support in the past took the center stage, leading the orchestra with solos or conversation pieces. The piano became the ruling instrument of the period, used for accompaniment and extensive soloing. The most celebrated romantic composers were obsessed by the piano and developed a new style of solo songs for the instrument.

During the nineteenth century, the guitar's shape evolved, its waist got thinner, and the tone improved to achieve clarity of sound onstage. The guitar didn't play a central role during the romantic years, even though the compositions requested an impressive technique.

Franz Schubert (1797–1828)

Franz Schubert was a man who loved life with no care for money. He composed music for his own pleasure and for his group of appreciative friends, with whom he had created the Schubertriads, a sort of social club centered around music. Schubert and his friend Johann Michael Vogl, a great singer of the time, would entertain guests with the numerous songs Schubert had composed, along with two symphonies and three masses, when he was a teacher at his father's school. Schubert, like many composers, owed his music education to his father and older brother. They taught him the violin, piano, organ, voice, and harmony, and later on sent him to master his studies with Antonio Salieri.

In 1818, Schubert became the music tutor of Count Esterházy's daughters. During this period, he composed a number of pieces on piano to be performed with four hands, along with the *Fifth Symphony* and the famous *Trout Quintet*. He had his work first published in 1821; that same year, he composed an opera long performed even after his death from syphilis in 1828.

He started to show the first symptoms of syphilis in 1822 and his health began to deteriorate, but he didn't lose his enthusiasm for life and composing. In fact, the last years of his life revealed his greatest musical genius. He wrote his most famous piece, the *String Quartet in A Minor* (the "Rosamunde" theme) in 1823. After 1825, publishers became interested in his work, and he started to become a renowned composer.

Just a small part of his work was published during his lifetime. Only after his death in 1828 and, more precisely, at the end of the nineteenth century did his inexhaustible and impressive work start to be printed and performed.

TWO ECOSSAISES

Music by Franz Schubert

Track 17

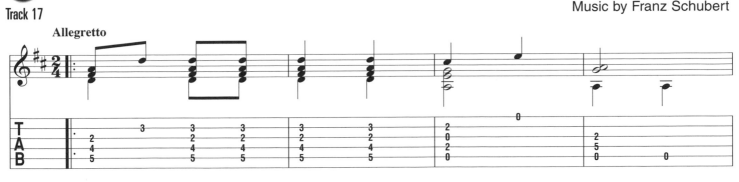

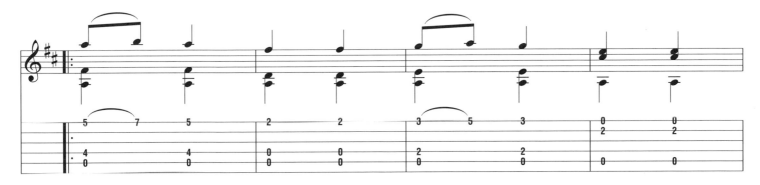

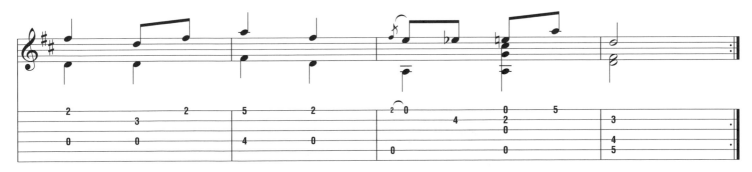

Johannes Brahms (1833–1897)

Brahms learned piano from his father at age seven and studied composition with Eduard Marzsen at age thirteen. He made a living from performing in taverns quite young and was the arranger for his father's orchestra. When playing with violinist Eduard Remenul in 1853, he met Liszt, along with Joseph Joachim, who would introduce him to his lifelong friend Robert Schumann. Schumann helped Brahms acquire his first publishing contract. After Schumann's death, Brahms became a devoted companion of the widow Clara Schumann, who was fourteen years older than him and one of the greatest pianists of the nineteenth century.

Brahms conducted a women's chorus in Hamburg and often spoke out against the new German school of music: the so-called "music of the future" led by Liszt and Wagner. He favored the idea of music composed for the love of music as a sole entity—not in support of theatrical play or ballet. Music had to be performed in its "absolute" form.

He settled in Vienna in 1868 after he failed to land a conducting position in Hamburg. He became famous with his masterpiece *German Requiem* (1869) and the *Variations on the St. Anthony Chorale* (1873). He is known for mastering the piano technique of variations displayed in "Variations on a Theme by Handel" (1862). From 1872 to 1885, he composed orchestral compositions, the symphonies in C minor and D major, a third and fourth symphony, a violin and piano concerto, and conducted the Society of the Friends of Music in Vienna. In 1891, he composed the *Quintet for Clarinet*, one of the best classical pieces ever written for clarinet, and the *Trio for Clarinet, Cello, and Piano*.

He died of cancer in 1897, one year after Clara Schumann's death.

WALTZ, OPUS 39, NO. 9

Track 18

Music by Johannes Brahms

Frederic Chopin (1810–1849)

Chopin was born in Poland in 1810 from a French father and an aristocratic Polish mother. He demonstrated a musical genius at a very young age when he started improvising his piano technique, even though he received classical piano lessons. His inventiveness is said to have been shaped around classical technique, but he did not follow the rules regarding what one was allowed or not allowed to play. By the age of eight, he had already developed an innovative playing style when he debuted as a brilliant performer at a charity event. A young prodigy, he published his first work at the age of fifteen, and by seventeen had established his reputation as a great performer.

He moved from Warsaw to Paris in 1830, after a failed Polish riot against the Russian occupation. There he met the famous Georges Sand, with whom he would have a passionate and much publicized affair. She was an eccentric writer who decided to publish her work under a male pseudonym.

Chopin was a worldly romantic musician respected by the high society and poets. His virtuosic piano improvisations impressed the Parisians, and the sophistication of his style influenced numbers of great composers, such as Liszt, Wagner, Debussy, Tchaikovsky, and Rachmaninov. He composed essentially for the piano and wrote numerous pieces, including mazurkas, preludes, polonaises, nocturnes, ballades, and sonatas. He would stay in Paris until the end of his life in 1849, when he died at age thirty-nine of tuberculosis.

PRELUDE, OPUS 28, NO. 7

Music by Frederic Chopin

Track 19

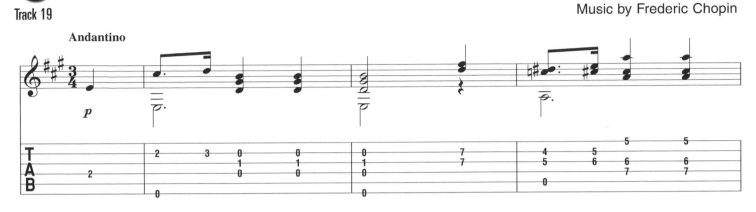

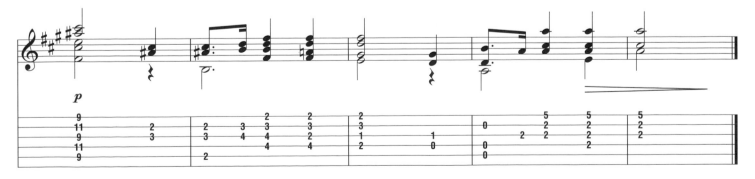

Robert Schumann (1810–1856)

Robert Schumann is one of the most important composers and leaders of the romantic movement in the nineteenth century. He started studying music at the age of eight and read books by his favorite writers in his father's bookshop in Zwickau, Germany.

He was multi-talented as a music critic, journalist, composer, and also a poet. Most of his life, he would place literature and music at the same level, and his versatility in the two media would help him survive his right-hand handicap. He lost the full use of his third finger in 1832 because of either a mercury treatment for a syphilis sore or the result of his overzealous use of a finger exercise machine.

When his father died in 1826, his mother pressured him to study law, but he decided instead to become a professional musician. He went on to study piano with Friedrich Wieck, whose daughter, Clara, he married in 1840. Clara was also a brilliant pianist and would give great performances of Schumann's work throughout her life.

Schumann concentrated on one certain style of music at a time. He had his lieder period and composed 140 of these art songs before he turned to orchestral music. He also went through a chamber music phase before becoming interested in choral music. Among his most important works are the "Abegg Variations," *Carnaval*, "Arabesque in C Major," *Piano Concerto in A Minor*, and his opera *Genoneva*.

He began to hallucinate from his illness in 1853 and suffered memory lapses that prevented him from conducting. In 1854 he began hearing voices and attempted suicide. He was put into a mental institution for the last two years of his life. Brahms, whom he admired, helped Clara through this difficult time. She was forbidden by the doctors to see her husband, for fear he would not take her visits well. Brahms became a devoted friend of hers for the rest of her life. She visited Schumann the day before he died in 1856.

MELODY

Track 20

Music by Robert Schumann

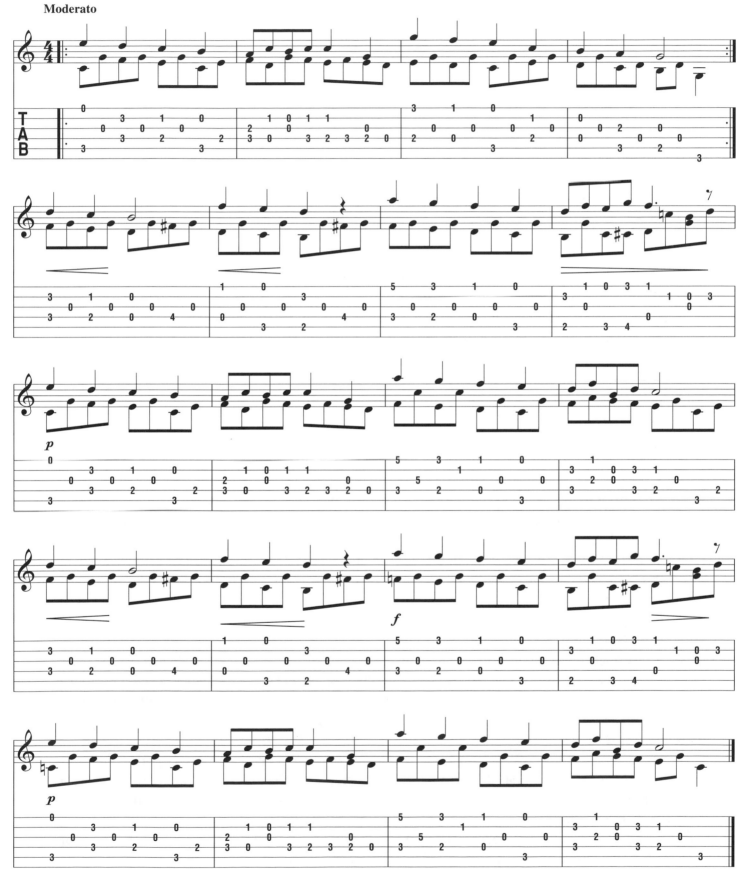

5 MODERN PERIOD (1910–)

Béla Bartók:	"Soliloquy"
Dmitri Shostakovich:	"March"
Erik Satie:	"Gymnopedie No. 3"
Piotr Tchaikovsky:	"Hymn"
Igor Stravinsky:	Excerpt from *The Five Fingers*

The modern years began with the impressionist painters, a movement that then spread to music. In reaction to the previous romantic period, the emphasis in music was no longer focused on emotions but rather on the senses and the intellect.

After World War I, music fragmented into several directions, while the Romantic school survived and evolved. Other composers experimented with new ideas of freedom. New sounds, new harmonies (Schoenberg's 12-tone style), and new technology helped to achieve these new trends with a wide range of instrumentation.

A traditional instrument like the guitar quickly took the center stage in the 1930s when Les Paul developed the first electric guitar with a solid body. Ten years later, Leo Fender added the first electric amplifier to his own custom guitars. The guitar became the major instrument of the century and boosted the advent of today's popular music. The audience of music lovers widened around the world to a level that was never seen in past history. This phenomenon, supported by the invention of new media like recording, radio, television, and films, helped to produce electric styles of music and accommodated the different tastes of each individual. Music is in a constant state of evolution, and, as Bartók once said, there is no end to the twelve notes.

Béla Bartók (1881–1945)

Béla Bartók is the greatest Hungarian composer ever and the most important composer of the twentieth century. He studied piano first with his mother and then with Istvan Thoman, and composition with Janos Koessler. Béla started composing around the age of nine. As a teenager, he listed to Brahms and Strauss. He wrote the symphonic poem *Kossuth* at age twenty-two, influenced by his admiration for Liszt and Strauss. After graduation from the Academy of Music in Budapest, he was offered a teaching position at the prestigious Hungarian school. At the same time, he established a reputation as a piano virtuoso through many concerts performed around the world.

In 1906, Bartók met Zoltan Kodály, and the two became lifelong friends. They shared the same interest in collecting folk songs from Hungary and surrounding countries. Together they published a catalog of *Hungarian Folksongs for Voice and Piano* (1906). Bartók collected and studied about 6,000 folk songs, which became a major influence on his compositions, along with the music of French composer Debussy. He used the ancient folk song harmonies and the 12-tone scale to create his unique and complex abstract style.

The *String Quartet No. 1* (1908), the ballet *The Wooden Prince* (1917), the opera *Blue Beard Castle* (1918), the dissonant ballet-pantomime *The Miraculous Mandarin* (1918), and his third and fourth string quartets (1927–1928) were masterpieces of twentieth century music and established him as a major modern composer.

Bartók married Márta Ziegler, with whom he had a son in 1910 (Béla Bartók, Jr.), but the marriage failed after fourteen years, and he married again in 1923 to pianist Ditta Pásztory. Together they had a son, Péter, born in 1924.

The thirties were Bartók's most prolific years, and the compositions reflected a search for new harmonies and dissonant intonations. He wrote many pieces for the piano, the most famous being *Piano Concerto No. 2* (1931) and the *Sonata for Two Pianos and Percussion* (1937). In 1940 he moved to New York in exile for political reasons. There he wrote his most popular works: the *Concerto for Orchestra* in 1943, and in 1944 the *Sonata for Solo Violin*, dedicated to Yehudi Menuhin. He died September 26, 1945, after a long battle with leukemia. He was buried in New York, but his son transferred his remains to Budapest in 1988, just before the collapse of the Berlin wall.

Track 21

SOLILOQUY

Music by Béla Bartók

Dmitri Shostakovich (1906–1975)

Dmitri Shostakovich graduated from the Petrograd Conservatory of Music in 1925 with his first symphony, which immediately established him as a major composer around the world. His symphony was performed in Leningrad, Berlin, and Philadelphia that same year. He studied piano at the age of eight with his mother, a professional pianist herself. His father was a government engineer, and his family supported the Soviet Revolution. In fact, Dmitri Shostakovich is the most famous Bolshevik composer—but it came with a price.

During the Lenin years of the twenties, he did not have too much trouble, as he was commissioned to compose for concert halls and the theater. His modern style was well regarded and respected. But in the thirties, Stalin's austere rigor influenced his composing. He was not allowed to compose as freely and had to censor himself in order to maintain peace under the strict Stalin dictatorship. Shostakovich was eventually condemned by Stalin as a decadent and frivolous musician. He had to wait until Stalin's death in 1953 to once again compose avant-garde pieces. This is not to say that during the Stalin years, he did not have the audacity to compose very dramatic pieces, expressing the misery of the Soviet people who had died by the millions for resisting communism.

He received numerous awards, both from the Soviet Union and abroad. A prolific composer with fifteen symphonies, fifteen string quartets, numerous movie scores, ballet, operas, chamber pieces, and piano solos, Dmitri Shostakovich died in Moscow in 1975 and was given a state burial. He is considered to be one of the most important composers of the twentieth century.

MARCH

Track 22

Music by Dmitri Shostakovich

Tempo di Marcia

Erik Satie (1866–1925)

Erik Satie was born in 1866 in Honfleur, a little French city in Normandie. Erik learned to play the piano at the age of seven and moved to Paris in his late teens to study music at the famous Paris Conservatory. He was known to be eccentric, both in his personal life as well as in his music. He had an obsessive personality and collected in his tiny studio numerous pieces of the same item. For example, he had one piano on top of another! His music reflected his compulsive temperament; his 1893 composition "Vexations" for piano made use of only 180 notes, but they were to be played 840 times! He was sarcastic about his music critics and loved to be provocative with his non-traditional way of composing. In 1903, he impressed them with his seven duets for piano titled *Three Pear-shaped Pieces*. He also gave derisive titles to his compositions, such as *Flabby Preludes for a Dog* (1912).

His early style was inspired by mediaeval music, but he quickly became an avant-garde composer, influencing the major composers of the twentieth century such as Debussy and Ravel, and the major artists of the Dadaist, Cubist, and Surrealistic periods: Picasso, Cocteau, Diaghilev, and Francis Picabia, among others. Not really known to the public during his lifetime, he emerged as a major composer in the 1960s when his work was finally recognized and widely recorded.

Erik Satie was an original who helped develop the shape of modern music—jazz included. He was the first to create the concept of ambient music in 1902 at a Parisian art gallery, which he mocked as "furniture music." He was poor but never sad about it and died a free spirit in Paris in 1925.

GYMNOPEDIE NO. 3

Track 23

Music by Erik Satie

Drop D tuning:
(low to high) D-A-D-G-B-E

Lento e grave

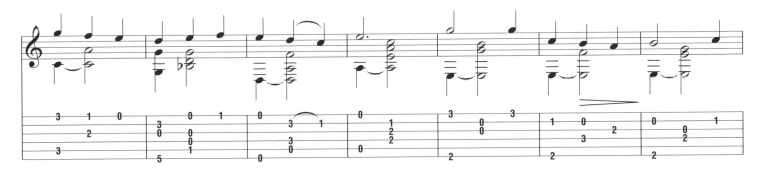

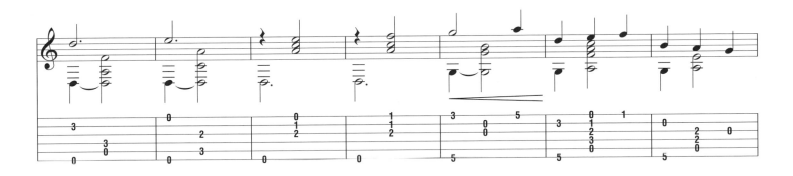

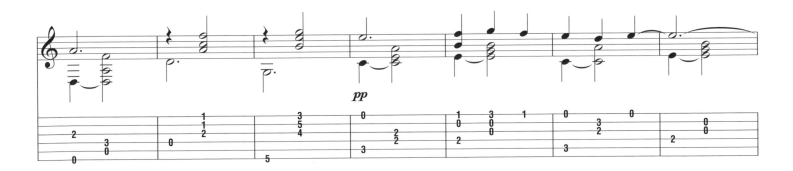

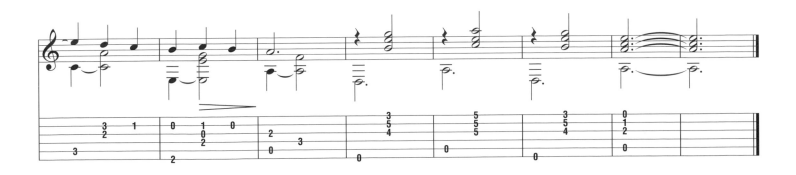

Piotr Tchaikovsky (1840–1893)

Tchaikovsky was the son of a mine inspector, but he demonstrated talent for the piano at the age of five and an incredible emotional sensitivity that would reveal to be the heart of his impressive composing. He studied music with the Kundinger brothers while studying law at the School of Jurisprudence. Like Schumann, Tchaikovsky would slowly decide that music was going to be the center of his life. He entered the St. Petersburg Conservatory of Music in 1862 and graduated with honors in 1865. He moved a year later to Moscow and worked for eleven years as music teacher at the newly opened Moscow Conservatory. During his time there, he composed memorable pieces, such as the overture-fantasia *Romeo and Juliet* in 1869 and the ballet *Swan Lake* in 1875.

He made the mistake of getting married in 1877 to one of his most fervent fans, even though he knew he was homosexual. The marriage immediately failed after nine weeks and an attempt at suicide. Afterward, he wrote three masterpieces: the *Fourth Symphony* (1877), the *Violin Concerto* (1878), and the famous opera *Eugene Onegin* (1877), which is, in part, based on his relationship with his wife.

In 1876, he began receiving financial support from Nadezhda von Meck that would last fourteen years. They practically never met but exchanged a voluminous and intimate correspondence. Her help, combined with that of Tzar Alexander III, allowed Tchaikovsky to quit teaching and devote himself entirely to composing and performing around Europe. He then composed the immensely famous ballet *Sleeping Beauty* (1889) and the intense opera *The Queen of Spades.* His fame as a conductor and composer grew internationally when he visited the United States in 1891, and he composed the beloved *Nutcracker* ballet in 1892. In 1893, Tchaikovsky died in St. Petersburg, nine days after the premier of his *Sixth Symphony*, either of cholera or a suicide.

HYMN

Track 24

Music by Piotr Tchaikovsky

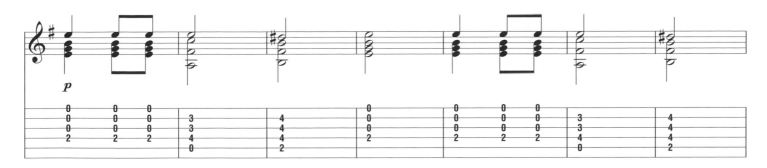

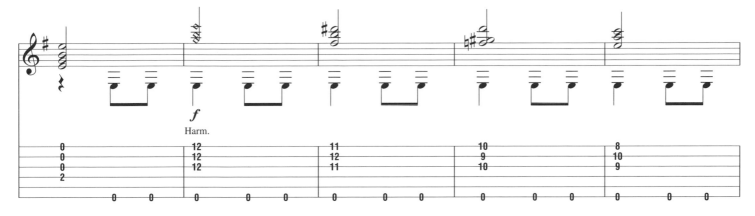

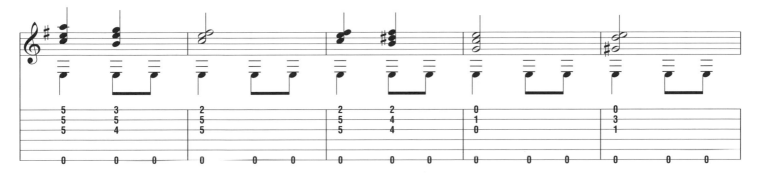

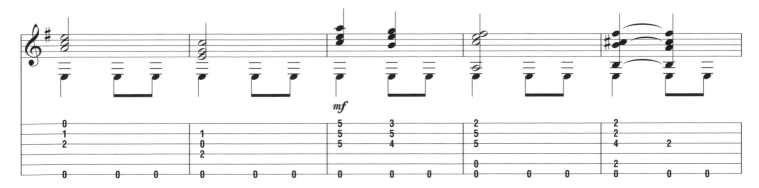

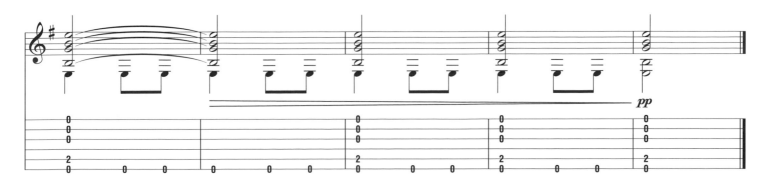

Igor Stravinsky (1882–1971)

The most influential composer of the twentieth century was born in a little Russian city near St. Petersburg in 1882. His father was an opera singer at the Mariinsky Theater in St. Petersburg. At first, Igor didn't take music seriously and was contemplating law as a source of income, until 1902, when he met Korsakov, with whom he studied composition. His early work was influenced by Tchaikovsky and Debussy but also by his love of folk songs. At the request of Diaghilev for his Ballet Russes, he composed the sensational *Firebird* (1910), *Petrushka* (1911), and the scandalous *The Rite of Spring* (1914), which created a near riot at the premiere. These three innovative masterpieces established Stravinsky at the age of thirty as a music revolutionary and a major composer of modern music.

Stravinsky left Russia for Paris in 1914, but shortly after moved to Switzerland to find peace during World War I. There he composed *l'Histoire du Soldat* (1918), written for seven instruments. After the war in 1920, he moved back to Paris for the premiere of his new ballet *Pulcinella* and renewed his collaboration with Diaghilev for the composition of the ballet *Oedipus Rex* in 1927.

In 1938, tragedy struck his family; one of his daughters, and a year later his wife and mother, died from tuberculosis. His second daughter also caught the disease and spent six years in a sanitarium. Stravinsky also got sick but survived after five months of intense care. That same year, he sadly decided to move to the United States, and a year later, in 1940, he chose Los Angeles as his new home with hopes of composing music for movies. He married a second time with his intimate friend since 1921, Véra de Bosset.

In Hollywood, he composed the *Symphony in Three Movements* (1945), which was intended for a movie score. Meanwhile, he had composed more ballets for the choreographer Balanchine, including *Apollon Musagète* (1928), *Jeux de Cartes*, (1936), *Orpheus* (1947), and the brilliant *Agon* (1957).

In 1947 Stravinsky was introduced to the music of Schoenberg and became very interested in his controversial 12-tone school of composition. The result is the astonishing serial style of *The Rake's Progress* (1951) and the even more astounding *Threni* (1958), which was influenced by Webern. He continued composing major works well into his eighties and died in New York in 1971. On his request, he was buried in Venice on the Island of San Michel close to his friend Diaghilev.

EXCERPT FROM "THE FIVE FINGERS"

Track 25

Music by Igor Stravinsky

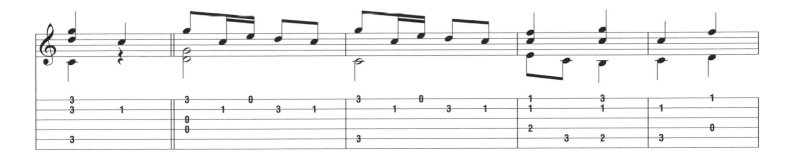

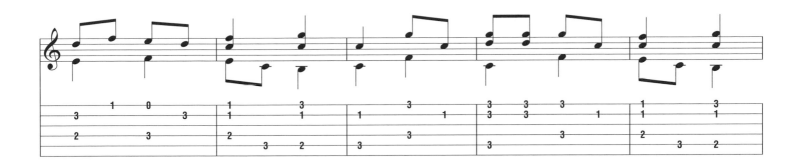

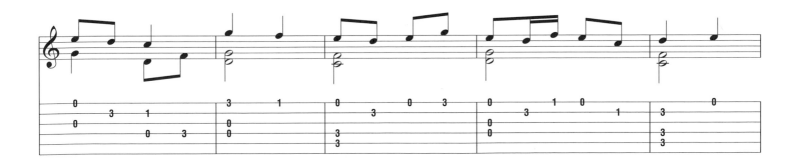

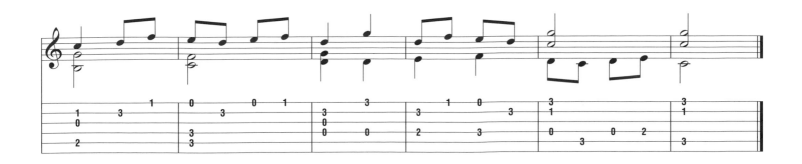

Acknowledgments and Dedication

Special Thanks to:

Marie-Christine Belkadi: for writing the text
Ernesto Homeyer: for editing the music charts
Jonathan Merkel: for recording, engineering, and producing this book
Danny Osuma: for the mastering
Danielle Welmond: for text editing
Chas Grasamke, Emilio Guim, Chris McCarthy, and Jesus Maria(epy) Garcia Rubio Polo Gonzalez Figueroa: for their support
Beth Marlis: from Musicians Institute
Joe Iacobellis: www.everlystrings.com
Jeff Schroedl: from Hal Leonard
Steve Blucher: from DiMarzio
Jude Gold: from Guitar Player

This book is dedicated to my wife, Marie-Christine Belkadi.